DECADES OF THE
20TH CENTURY

The 1930s

From the Great Depression to The Wizard of Oz

Stephen Feinstein

E **Enslow Publishers, Inc.**

40 Industrial Road   PO Box 38
Box 398   Aldershot
Berkeley Heights, NJ 07922   Hants GU12 6BP
USA   UK
http://www.enslow.com

Library of Congress Cataloging-in-Publication Data

Feinstein, Stephen.
     The 1930s from the Great Depression to the Wizard of Oz / Stephen Feinstein.
          p. cm. — (Decades of the 20th century)
     Includes bibliographical references and index.
     ISBN 0-7660-1609-9
     1. United States—Civilization—1918–1945—Juvenile literature. 2. Nineteen thirties—Juvenile literature.   [1. Nineteen thirties. 2. United States.—History—1919–1933. 3. United States.—History—1933–1945. 4. United States.—Social life and customs—1918–1945.]   I. Title. II. Series: Feinstein, Stephen. Decades of the 20th century.
E169.1.F355   2001
973.9—dc21
                                        00-010054

Printed in the United States of America

10 9 8 7 6 5 4 3 2

Illustration Credits: Associated Press, p. 32B; Bert Randolph Sugar, *The Great Baseball Players from McGraw to Mantle* (Mineola, N.Y.: Dover Publications, Inc., 1997), p. 30; © Corel Corporation, pp. 52, 55, 56, 61; Courtesy of the Babe Didrikson Zaharias Foundation, pp. 1, 31; *The Depression Years, As Photographed by Arthur Rosenstein* (New York: Dover Publications, Inc., 1978), pp. 2T, 3B, 5, 6, 18, 26B, 40; Enslow Publishers, Inc., p. 18; Franklin D. Roosevelt Library, pp. 2B, 20; Library of Congress, pp. 1, 4, 7, 8, 9, 11, 12, 13, 15, 22, 25, 26T, 27, 28, 29, 33, 34, 37, 39, 41, 42, 43, 44, 46, 47, 58, 59, 60T, 61; *Movie Star Postcards*, © 1986 Dover Publications, Inc., pp. 1, 3T, 19, 23, 24, 60; National Aeronautics and Space Administration, p. 53; National Archives, pp. 21, 32T, 35, 38, 50–51, 51T, 57; National Archives, Washington, D.C., Courtesy of the United States Holocaust Memorial Museum, p. 48; New Jersey State Police, pp. 14, 61; Stella Blum, *Everyday Fashions of the Thirties, As Pictured in Sears Catalogs* (New York: Dover Publications, Inc., 1986), p. 16; U.S. Holocaust Museum Photo Archives, pp. 45, 60.

Cover Illustrations: © Corel Corporation; Library of Congress; *Movie Star Postcards*, © 1986 Dover Publications, Inc.

Contents

The 1920s, a decade known as the Roaring Twenties, had been a time of great prosperity in America. But then came the crash of the New York stock market in the fall of 1929—and suddenly, the party was over. As the 1930s dawned, Americans faced a collapsing economy. The Great Depression threw millions out of work. To make matters worse, a severe drought made it impossible for many farmers to grow crops. Hundreds of thousands of families were forced to give up their farms. Many headed west to find work, and became migrant farmers in California.

By the start of the 1930s, the Great Depression was already in full swing. The days of the Roaring Twenties, when flappers danced wildly (opposite) and people seemed to be enjoying themselves all the time, were over.

The Depression threw many people not only out of work, but out of their homes. Below, police enforce an eviction of sharecroppers from their home.

At first, President Herbert Hoover did not seem to see how big the problem was. On March 7, 1930, he promised that the Depression would be over in sixty days. Instead, the country sank deeper into the Depression. One by one, businesses failed. The unemployed searched in vain for new jobs. Some sold apples on street corners. Others begged. Families were faced with the threat of starvation. Banks failed and many customers lost their life's savings. In 1932, Americans, eager for change, elected Franklin Delano Roosevelt as the next president.

Roosevelt ushered in a new era of hope. He began government programs to pull the country out of the Depression. Known as the New Deal, these relief efforts would radically change the role of the federal government in the lives of the American people.

5

A Scrap of Bread, a Bowl of Soup

Every day, millions of Americans in cities and towns all over the country waited patiently in long breadlines at local soup kitchens. There, they would receive a bowl of soup and a bit of bread. Soup kitchens were the only source of food some people had. In remote locations such as the mountain towns of Appalachia, where there were no soup kitchens, some families survived by eating dandelions and blackberries.

As more people lost their jobs, the breadlines grew longer. Still, some did not admit that something was terribly wrong. President Herbert Hoover kept trying to reassure the nation that everything would be fine. "No one is actually starving," he proclaimed. In the fall of 1930, Hoover created the President's Emergency Committee for Employment (PECE). It did little beyond issuing misleading reports about the adequacy of local relief efforts. Hoover, a self-made millionaire, sincerely believed that any further government attempts to fix what he saw as a "temporary setback" in the economy would only hurt America's greatness. He and others like him believed America was built on hard work, honesty, and the independence of the individual.

By May 1931, however, Hoover could no longer ignore the crisis. Still, he did not want the federal government to lend a helping hand. Hoover thought government charity would rob people of the motivation to take care of themselves. "The way to the nation's

The image of the apple vendor, selling fruit at roadside stands (opposite), is one of the most enduring of the Great Depression era.

President Hoover (above, at right) and many of his advisors, including Treasury Secretary Andrew Mellon (above, left), believed the government should do nothing about the Great Depression. Ups and downs were inevitable in business, they thought, and the economy could regulate itself.

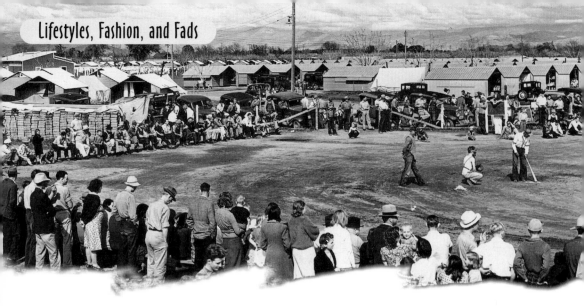

Although the huge wandering, homeless population consisted mostly of men, among them were also young girls, pregnant women, young couples, and even some senior citizens. Some found homes in makeshift shantytowns, where life was hard. Still, many found ways to have fun, like these people (above) playing baseball in the middle of their Hooverville.

Aviator Amelia Earhart (opposite, with her plane below her) gave Americans hope for the future with her brave flights around the world.

greatness is the path of self-reliance," he said. He called for acts of charity by individuals and private enterprise to solve the nation's problems. One citizen who heeded Hoover's request was gangster Al "Scarface" Capone, who set up a soup kitchen in Chicago.

Hoovervilles and Boxcars

Hundreds of thousands of Americans suddenly found themselves homeless. They drifted into a nomadic (wandering) way of life. They took to riding the rails, "hopping" freight trains in search of better opportunities in the next town or state. Almost a quarter of a million of these people were teenagers who had become transients when their schools shut down. The number of people on the move was staggering. Officials of the Southern Pacific Railroad claimed to have thrown almost seven hundred thousand rail riders off their trains in just one year!

Meanwhile, thousands of other homeless Americans chose to stay in their hometowns. They slept in doorways, on park benches, underneath bridges, or in abandoned cars. Many went to the outskirts of town, where they created communities of shanties. They built shelters out of any available material such as cardboard or scraps of wood. These communities of the homeless came to be called "Hoovervilles." The nickname showed the growing anger at the Hoover administration's failure to take action to solve the nation's problems.

Into the Wild Blue Yonder

While millions of Americans during the 1930s were spiraling downward, Amelia Earhart was soaring skyward. She had learned to fly in 1920 and quickly developed a passion for flying. In 1928, Earhart was a passenger on a flight across the Atlantic Ocean. Then, in 1932, she became the first woman to fly solo across the Atlantic, making the trip from Harbor Grace, Newfoundland, to Ireland in fifteen and a half hours.

Earhart continued to set new records in the sky, twice breaking the women's speed record for a flight from Los Angeles to New York. In 1935, she flew from Hawaii to California, the first person ever to make such a flight.

In 1937, Earhart planned to fly around the world. She took off from Miami with her navigator, Frank Noonan. Sadly, this was her last flight. After completing about three quarters of the planned route, Earhart's plane went down over the Pacific Ocean and disappeared without a trace. America mourned the loss of this pioneer of the sky, whose courage had lifted the spirits of her fellow Americans.

Down on the Farm

While urban Americans in the early 1930s were suddenly forced to deal with a collapsing economy, America's farmers had been suffering financial decline since 1922. Huge surpluses had driven down the prices of agricultural products. Throughout the 1920s, agricultural exports, crop prices, and land values were in a constant decline. During those years, farm families—then about 25 percent of America's population—struggled to maintain their rural lifestyle. They continued to hope that things would someday get better. But when the 1930s arrived, things got much worse.

President Hoover realized that farmers were in trouble. One of his first acts as president was to call Congress into session in April 1929 to create a program to help farmers. The Agricultural Marketing Act set up a Federal Farm Board to help farm cooperatives (business organizations owned by workers) at local, state, and regional levels. The board bought and stored crops from the farmers. Hoover believed that farmers could best help themselves with cooperatives. Unfortunately, the program did not work. The farmers' situation continued to get worse.

The Dust Bowl

The Great Plains had always experienced periods of drought. The drought that began in the early 1930s and continued through most of the decade was remarkable only because of its severity. A combination of factors would create the "Dust Bowl"— the worst environmental disaster in United States history. As the farmlands dried out, raising crops became very difficult. Adding to the problem was the fact that many farmers had overcultivated their lands. Grass had disappeared in many places, plowed under by farmers or eaten by cattle. When gusty winds began to blow

over the Great Plains, the top layer of dried-out soil, no longer held down by grass, blew away. This airborne soil formed thick clouds of dust. Walls of dust, sometimes rising as high as five miles into the air, swept across the farmlands and cities of the Midwest, turning day into night and often burying farm animals, cars, and even houses.

Thousands of farmers had been forced off the land due to financial problems even before the dust came. When Dust Bowl conditions developed, hundreds of thousands more farm families were forced to abandon their farms. The roads leading west became clogged with the worn-out vehicles of migrating farm families.

Those without vehicles had to walk. Because many of them came from Oklahoma, they came to be called Okies. Writer John Steinbeck vividly portrayed their desperation in his 1939 novel *The Grapes of Wrath*. Many of the Okies who reached California found work as migrant farmers. They were often exploited by the wealthy landowners. Living conditions were awful, work was hard, and pay was low. A migrant worker was paid ten cents for each fifty-pound box of figs he or she picked, and most could

The Dust Bowl destroyed farms in widespread areas. Crops were ruined and the land became too barren to support more growth. Even more dangerous were the swirling dust storms (above) that could choke people and animals and bury valuable equipment.

11

Many Americans, especially those thrown out of their homes, were not fortunate enough to have access to a soup kitchen. These people had to fend for themselves, begging for food and often fighting over scraps in garbage cans. Others simply took to the road with all their belongings (above), hoping to find a better life in other places, such as California and Oregon.

pick no more than three boxes a day. About thirty dollars was the most a worker could earn per season.

Many farmers in other parts of the country did not have to abandon their farms. They continued to produce extra crops, but this kept prices—and income—low. Finally, some help arrived. When Franklin D. Roosevelt became president in 1933, he created the Agricultural Adjustment Administration (AAA). The AAA paid farmers to reduce the size of their crops, thereby driving up the prices of agricultural goods. Ironically, because Dust Bowl conditions contributed to the reduction in crops, it also had the beneficial effect of driving up prices of farm products. By 1936, American farmers' income had increased by about 50 percent.

Another federal government program, the Soil Conservation Service (SCS), was established in 1935 to teach farmers how to protect the soil and slow the erosion process. The SCS, through a program called the Shelterbelt Project, planted trees in various parts of the Great Plains to serve as windbreaks, thereby helping to prevent Dust Bowl conditions from developing in the future.

Crime Pays, for a While

The Eighteenth Amendment banning the manufacture and sale of alcoholic beverages had been added to the Constitution in 1919. As a result, organized crime in America had grown powerful. "Bootlegging," or the sale of illegal alcohol, had become a big business. Throughout the 1920s and early 1930s, the "mob," led by gangsters such as Al Capone, had provided alcohol to those Americans willing to defy Prohibition by going to illegal bars, or "speakeasies." When the government ended Prohibition in 1933 by repealing the Eighteenth Amendment, the mob had to find other ways to get rich.

As the Depression descended on the country in the early 1930s, other criminals captured the attention of the public. For a while, some Americans viewed bank robbers as romantic outlaws striking back at a system that had failed them. As a crime wave swept the nation, newspapers were filled with stories of criminals such as Bonnie Parker and Clyde Barrow, "Pretty Boy" Floyd, "Baby Face" Nelson, and John Dillinger.

During the early 1930s, Hollywood producers churned out gangster movies such as *The Public Enemy* (1931) starring James Cagney. But as the crime

During Prohibition, police rounded up many bottles of illegal alcohol (bottom). In the 1920s, many Americans grew tolerant of criminals in the bootlegging business, associating them with the glamour and excitement of the speakeasy scene.

Al Capone (left), sometimes called "Scarface," was one of the best-known gangsters of the Prohibition era. He became famous not only for his violent criminal activities, but for his numerous attempts to help his community. He opened soup kitchens, and during the Lindbergh baby kidnapping case, he offered to try to find out information about the kidnapping from other members of the underworld.

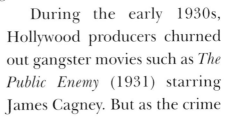

Charles A. Lindbergh (below, left) first made headlines in 1927, when he became the first man to fly solo nonstop across the Atlantic Ocean. When his son Charles, Jr., was kidnapped and murdered in 1932, the elder Lindbergh was one of the most famous men in the world. It was partly his fame that made the case, in which Bruno Hauptmann (below, right) was convicted and executed for the crime, so sensational.

wave continued, the public's tolerance began to fade. Too many innocent victims had been killed during holdups and bank robberies. One by one, the famous bank robbers were either caught or killed by the police.

Other crimes, such as kidnapping, were also on the rise. In the most sensational case, the baby son of famous aviator Charles Lindbergh and his wife, Anne, was kidnapped and murdered. In a controversial trial, Bruno Richard Hauptmann was convicted and executed for the crime.

Hope for a Better Tomorrow

Americans in the 1930s needed a dose of optimism to help them deal with life in the Depression. That spark of hope came about in the form of several World's Fairs. The largest took place in Chicago and New York. In

1933–1934, the Chicago World's Fair, called the "Century of Progress Exposition," focused on progress in science and technology that had occurred since the founding of Chicago in 1833. More than 39 million visitors were encouraged to view their current economic difficulties from a long-term perspective. The exhibits proved that America's course was onward and upward.

The New York World's Fair of 1939–1940 was called "The World of Tomorrow." This exposition presented a vision of a fabulous future life of ease and prosperity. Machines such as Elektro the Talking Robot would do much of the work. And a fantastic invention called television would allow people to experience faraway sights and sounds in the comfort of their own living rooms. To many Americans, it seemed as though these concepts had been borrowed from the world of Buck Rogers, a science-fiction comic strip hero of the time.

The 1939 World's Fair was held in Flushing Meadow, New York. Its theme was a celebration of progress and hope for the future of science and technology, as can be seen in this futuristic advertising poster (above) for the fair. Among the many "futuristic" inventions displayed for the first time at the fair was the television.

Simple, Elegant, and Reusable

A new look in women's fashion emerged in the 1930s in America. In response to the economic crisis, designers created clothing that was more affordable and that featured a quality of timeless elegance in contrast to the flamboyant "flapper" look of the 1920s. Hemlines were longer, and slim waistlines were emphasized. Typical, practical, everyday women's wear consisted of a simple print dress, belted just above the hips and falling five inches below the knee. Women's shoes had lower heels. Women

15

tended to use less makeup, preferring a more natural look. Toward the end of the decade, broader shoulders became popular in both women's and men's clothing. The wide padded shoulders contrasted dramatically with narrow waistlines.

Because of hard times, women now wore the same dresses from one season to the next, instead of buying new outfits. Accessories such as hats, pocketbooks, shoes, gloves, and jewelry—especially costume jewelry—became more important. The accessories created the impression of a new "look" while the woman wore the same dress or suit on different occasions.

While most Americans coped as best as they could during the Great Depression, saving money when it came to clothing, America's wealthy threw lavish parties and debutante balls. The women of high society continued to buy fancy outfits from top designers in Paris. But the fact that most American women could no longer afford expensive clothing created an opportunity for American designers, such as Elizabeth Hawes, to produce affordable yet stylish outfits. In 1932, a woman could buy a checkered dress and dark coat combination designed by Hawes for $10.75, one tenth the cost of her custom pieces. Meanwhile, in Hollywood, costume designer Adrian was creating elegant clothes for stars such as Marlene Dietrich, Joan Crawford, and Greta Garbo. Adrian's styles would influence other American designers, who were responding to the American woman's interest in the fashion styles of the stars.

Simplicity of style was the rule in women's fashions of the 1930s. Dresses (above) were neatly tailored in comparison to the earlier flapper look. Accessories, such as new hats (below), became important. Sometimes a new accessory was all a women could afford to change the "look" of her wardrobe from season to season.

The Year of Get-Rich-Quick Schemes

Many Americans had had their hopes and dreams wrecked by the Depression. Others were forced to live with lowered expectations for achieving financial security. It is no wonder that so many were captivated by a board game called Monopoly, which first became available in 1935. Players could, for a moment, become rich beyond their wildest dreams—at least in their imaginations. Another game, Bingo, also appeared in 1935. Although some criticized it as a legal form of gambling, it became popular all over the country. At least in this game, one could win real money.

Perhaps the most popular get-rich-quick scheme was the chain letter. In the spring of 1935, the first chain letters began arriving. The source of the letters is unknown. But before long, millions of Americans around the country were caught up in the frenzy of a new national craze. Those who received a letter frantically scratched out the name at the top of the list of six names, added their own name at the bottom, and mailed the letter, along with a dime, to the person whose name had been at the top of the list. Chain-letter participants expected to receive a payment of 15,625 dimes once the letter had been passed along by five more people. But the scheme did not work. Still, post offices around the nation were so overwhelmed by the millions of chain letters that they had to hire extra help. Eventually, the excitement faded when people failed to receive their $1,562.50 in the mail.

Putting the Pieces Together

In their spare time, Americans spent countless hours bent over tables trying to fit together the pieces of jigsaw puzzles. The first puzzles in the early 1930s were made of plywood, and they were

expensive. But by 1934, inexpensive jigsaw puzzles were being made out of heavy cardboard. Within a few months, 3.5 million jigsaw puzzles had been distributed. Those who could not afford to buy jigsaw puzzles could rent them. The jigsaw puzzle craze swept the nation and continued throughout the rest of the decade. As one avid puzzle fan put it, "I like puzzles because when I put them together I don't have to think."

Dimples and Curls

When Americans in the 1930s saw Shirley Temple in her first starring role in *Stand Up and Cheer* (1934), they went wild over the five-year-old Hollywood star. Perhaps her innocent smiling face, with her dimples and curly hair, evoked memories of happier times, which audiences of the 1930s must have yearned for. Americans could not get enough of the little actress. Soon, her face was appearing on books, ribbons, and buttons. Americans bought millions of Shirley Temple dolls and coloring books, and Shirley Temple look-alike contests were held throughout the country. A nonalcoholic cocktail, made from ginger ale and a dash of grenadine and served with a maraschino cherry, was even named after her, and it became popular with young people.

The Depression had brought many Americans face to face with many terrible problems they could not solve. Perhaps that is why so many were drawn to jigsaw puzzles (opposite), which provided them with a problem they could solve.

Shirley Temple (below), perhaps the greatest child star in the history of America, retired from her acting career in 1949. The next year, she married Charles Black, then went on to become a representative in the United Nations General Assembly and later an ambassador. She was also the first woman to serve as chief of protocol in the State Department.

After being elected in 1932, President Roosevelt went to work to try to end the Great Depression. The programs he started were called the New Deal. While trying to help the ordinary American citizen, the Roosevelt administration also increased government regulation of banking and business. Safety-net measures, such as Social Security, were put into place.

President Franklin Roosevelt (opposite) impressed people with his strength, optimism, and confidence, giving many Americans hope for a future beyond the Great Depression.

The New Deal put many people back to work, even if some critics complained it was menial busywork. Below, a group of WPA workers are in the process of improving a street in Indianapolis in 1934.

A New Deal for the Arts

As part of his New Deal, President Roosevelt set up a work-relief agency known as the Works Progress Administration (WPA). The WPA paid for about 125,000 public buildings, such as post offices, to be built and created more than 8 million jobs in the process. The Federal Art Project (FAP), a part of the WPA, paid for art projects—murals, paintings, and sculptures—often to decorate the new public buildings built by the WPA. By 1939, FAP-funded muralists, painters, and sculptors had completed 1,300 murals, 48,100 paintings, and more than 3,500 sculptures.

The huge new murals often depicted the struggles of the working class in a style known as social realism. Many of the artists were influenced by the great Mexican muralist Diego Rivera. Among the artists employed by the FAP were Thomas Hart Benton, Grant Wood, and Jackson Pollock. Other WPA art programs included the Federal Theatre Project, the Federal Writers Project, and the Federal Music Project. All of these New Deal programs put artists to work producing government-sponsored books, music, and shows.

Mexican painter Diego Rivera was a big influence on the people aided by the Federal Artists Project. His early work was part of the school of social realism. Later, he worked in the cubist style (right). His art often focused on the struggle of the working class.

Bela Lugosi (opposite, top right), one of the most popular actors of the decade, starred as Dracula in the film of the same name. Among the other films that were well-received during the 1930s was Frankenstein, starring Boris Karloff (opposite, left), another horror film that helped people escape the reality of the Great Depression. Also popular were gangster films, such as Little Caesar, starring Edward G. Robinson (opposite, bottom).

Forget Your Troubles

What could be a more pleasant way to spend an afternoon than attending a matinee at the local movie theater? For the unemployed, movies provided a perfect escape from boredom and despair——at least for a couple of hours. This escape was possible, of course, if one had the twenty-five-cent price of admission.

Millions of Americans flocked to the movies during the Depression, and Hollywood provided a wide choice of fantasies—horror films such as *Dracula* (1931) starring Bela Lugosi, *Frankenstein* (1931) starring Boris Karloff, and *King Kong* (1933). There were also lavish musicals, such as *42nd Street* (1933) with elaborate dance numbers directed by Busby Berkeley, and *Flying Down to Rio* (1933) with Fred Astaire and Ginger Rogers. Gangster movies such as *Little Caesar* (1930) starring Edward G. Robinson were popular, as were comedies

The Wizard of Oz (below), starring, from left to right, Jack Haley, Judy Garland, and Ray Bolger, showcased the latest in cinematic advances, particularly color. It captured the imaginations of Americans everywhere, and remains one of the best loved films of all time.

such as *Duck Soup* (1933) starring the Marx brothers. People enjoyed Westerns such as *Stagecoach* (1939) starring John Wayne, mystery films such as *The Thin Man* (1934) starring William Powell and Myrna Loy, and adventure films such as *Mutiny on the Bounty* (1935) starring Charles Laughton.

In 1935, *Becky Sharp*, the first feature-length movie filmed in a color process called Technicolor, was released. Although the color was far from perfect, audiences who were used to films in black and white were amazed by the new element of realism. In 1938, Walt Disney released the animated film *Snow White and the Seven Dwarfs*, his first feature-length cartoon. The following year, two of the most popular movies of all time were released: the musical fantasy *The Wizard of Oz* starring Judy Garland, and the Civil War epic *Gone With the Wind*, starring Clark Gable and Vivien Leigh.

Hours of Listening Pleasure

When they were not watching movies, Americans turned to another immensely popular entertainment—the radio. The 1930s were truly the golden age of radio. Radio listeners could find just about any type of entertainment they wanted. There were all kinds of romance, mystery, and adventure shows. The art of sound effects was perfected so that audiences listening to a couple of coconut shells on a soundboard believed they heard the hooves of the Lone Ranger's horse, Silver. The airwaves were also filled with all kinds of music, including live broadcasts from the Metropolitan Opera in New York and the NBC Symphony Orchestra conducted by Arturo Toscanini, as well as popular swing bands and jazz singers. Comedians such as George Burns and Gracie Allen, Jack Benny, and Ed Wynn became radio stars. Sports broadcasts were also very popular, as were quiz shows and amateur hours.

The 1930s represented the peak of radio's popularity. Just about every American household had a radio (above) as the centerpiece of entertainment in the living room. Families gathered daily to listen to the many programs offered, which ranged from soap opera dramas to Wild West action adventures.

Invaders From Mars

By the mid-1930s, radio stations began broadcasting the news. Millions of Americans got into the habit of relying on their local radio stations, in addition to newspapers, for information. Perhaps that is why the reaction of hundreds of thousands of Americans to Orson Welles's radio broadcast of H. G. Wells's 1898 novel *The War of the Worlds* should not have been so surprising.

On Sunday evening, October 30, 1938, Orson Welles, on the radio program Mercury Theater on the Air, began describing a frightful event—the landing of Martian invaders in New Jersey! Most listeners had missed the introductory comments stating that the broadcast was an adaptation of a work of fiction. They believed that the shocking report they were hearing was an actual news report. Widespread panic occurred in various parts of the country, as Welles related details about the Martians' weapons and their power. Because the broadcast terrified so many Americans, CBS radio had to agree never again to broadcast a make-believe news event.

Producer Orson Welles (above) stunned America when he broadcast his radio interpretation of H. G. Wells's War of the Worlds *in 1938.*

Young people especially enjoyed dancing the wild moves of the jitterbug (right) to the popular swing songs of the time.

Jitterbugging With the King of Swing

Jazz clarinet player Benny Goodman watched in amazement from the bandstand as the energetic couples on the dance floor threw themselves with wild abandon into the intricate steps of the jitterbug, the new dance that was sweeping the nation. Goodman marveled at the athletic steps of the dance partners who at times seemed more like acrobats than dancers. Goodman later said, "Their eyes popped, their heads pecked, their feet tapped out the time, arms jerked to the rhythm."

In the mid-1930s, Goodman, who came to be called the "King of Swing," and other bandleaders, such as Tommy Dorsey, Glenn Miller, Count Basie, and Duke Ellington, played a style of jazz known as swing. Live radio broadcasts helped make the music popular. Featuring sophisticated big-band arrangements, swing was not only good to listen to, it was also great dance music. For the next ten years, swing would be the most popular kind of music in America. Jazz singers who appeared with the bands, such as Ella Fitzgerald, Helen O'Connell, and Billie Holiday, also became popular.

After winning an amateur talent contest in Harlem, New York, in 1935, jazz singer Ella Fitzgerald (below) went on to become one of the best singers in the history of jazz music. Known for her beautiful voice with its broad range, she was also famous for her ability to improvise through scat singing in which wordless syllables are sung rhythmically instead of lyrics.

Racism and "Strange Fruit"

When African-American singer Billie Holiday went on the road as a jazz vocalist with Artie Shaw's all-white band, she was often the target of racism, especially in the South. Intolerance and hatred against minorities remained an ugly reality in many places. During the 1930s in the South, acts of racist brutality were still occurring. There were incidents of African Americans being lynched (killed as punishment for an alleged crime without a trial) each year. In one famous case in Scottsboro, Alabama, in 1931, nine young African-American men who were falsely accused of raping

two white women were nearly lynched by a mob. But the officials prevented this and the nine stood trial. All were convicted of the crime. Eight were sentenced to death, and the other—a twelve-year-old—was given a life sentence. Ultimately, after years of legal battles, the convictions were overturned. But other African Americans in similar situations were not so "lucky."

In 1939, twenty-four-year-old Billie Holiday recorded a song called "Strange Fruit." It was her personal protest against racism and lynching. The lyrics, written by poet Lewis Allen, began:

> *Southern trees bear a strange fruit*
> *Blood on the leaves and blood at the root*
> *Black body swinging in the Southern breeze*
> *Strange fruit hanging from the poplar trees*

The Two "Babes"

One of the most popular diversions for Americans in the Great Depression was sports, and the favorite sport continued to be America's favorite pastime—baseball. In 1932, New York Yankees baseball star George Herman "Babe" Ruth's fabulous career was winding down as he played in his last World Series, against the Chicago Cubs. Americans would miss Babe Ruth's home runs.

But there was another "Babe" in American sports, a woman whose career was about to take off in 1932. She could play baseball, basketball, football, tennis, and golf. She also excelled at swimming and track and field. She even boxed. When it came to sports, there was

not much that Mildred "Babe" Didrikson could not do. Because she was such an amazing all-around athlete, it seemed a pretty safe bet that she would put on an impressive performance in the 1932 summer Olympics in Los Angeles. Earlier that year, Didrikson entered eight of ten events in the National Women's Track and Field Championships. There, she won five events and tied one. At the Olympics, she won a gold medal in the javelin throw and in the eighty-meter hurdles, setting world records in both events. Americans were proud of their new Olympic star.

Known as the first great home-run hitter in professional baseball, Babe Ruth (opposite) also became famous for his colorful personality. He set many records—such as his 2,056 career walks and the 72 games in which he hit two or more home runs. Over the course of his career, Ruth had a .342 lifetime batting average.

Babe Didrikson (left) won a silver medal instead of gold in the high jump in the 1932 Olympics. Although she jumped a record five feet five and a quarter inches, she went over the bar head first. Despite her ability, Didrikson was not on the 1936 Olympic team. The United States Amateur Athletic Association had ruled that she was no longer an amateur because she had appeared in a car advertisement. She was disqualified from participating.

Jesse Owens Teaches Hitler a Lesson

During the Depression, some hopeless people who felt they had nothing to lose considered replacing the American system of government. Other models were available, including fascism in Germany. In some places in Europe, people eager for change threw their support behind power-hungry dictators, believing their promises and accepting their lies.

The 1936 summer Olympics were held in Berlin. Germany's dictator, Adolf Hitler, hoped to use the Olympics to win a major propaganda victory for his Nazi beliefs. Hitler's wish was for Germany's athletes to walk away with all the gold medals, proving to the world the superiority of their so-called "Aryan" race. Hitler asked his personal filmmaker, Leni Riefenstahl, to document the Nazi victories at the games.

Athletes from many countries had mixed feelings about going to Berlin. Hitler had already begun his persecution of Jews in Germany and had made known his racist views regarding other peoples. But the athletes had spent years of hard work training for the Olympics, and they chose to participate.

Adolf Hitler (above, top left), who claimed that his own Aryan race was superior to others, especially Jews and blacks, refused to congratulate Jesse Owens (below) on his Olympic victories. Owens did the 100-meter dash in a record 10.3 seconds and the 200-meter dash in 20.7 seconds. He did the long jump in 26 feet 5.5 inches, and he and his teammates completed the 400-meter relay in 39.8 seconds. So much for Aryan superiority!

Before the United States Olympic Committee agreed to American participation in the games, it received Hitler's guarantee that there would be no discrimination against African-American or Jewish-American athletes. Ultimately, 328 athletes from the United States went to Berlin. Among them were ten African Americans and many Jews.

Hitler's plan to score a propaganda victory back-fired. Jesse Owens, an African-American athlete, won four gold medals and was named "Athlete of the Games." Owens proved to be the most popular figure of the 1936 Olympics. The ten United States African-American athletes walked away with a total of eight gold, three silver, and two bronze medals. Hitler did not bother to stick around and congratulate Jesse Owens and his teammates.

Boxer Joe Louis won the Amateur Association Light Heavyweight Championship in 1934, the year he became a professional. He won his first twenty-three matches, before he lost in 1936 to former heavyweight champion Max Schmeling (below), who held the title from 1930–1932. Louis won back the championship in June 1937 by knocking out James J. Braddock.

The Golden Age of Boxing

Because boxing was illegal in many areas of the United States at the turn of the twentieth century, it had fewer fans than most other sports. In 1920, however, New York legalized boxing, and was soon followed by other states. By the 1930s, boxing had not only become a popular spectator sport, but was in a "golden age" of popularity.

Perhaps the most famous boxer of the 1930s was Joe Louis. He became the heavyweight champion when he defeated James J. Braddock in June 1937. He defend-ed his heavyweight title twenty-five times, holding the title longer than any other boxer, from 1937 until he retired in 1949.

By 1932, millions of Americans had lost their jobs. Many had lost their homes as well. Among the huge number of unemployed were veterans of World War I. In appreciation for their service to their country, in 1924 Congress had passed a bill promising the veterans a cash bonus. They would not receive it, however, until 1945. During the Great Depression, realizing that many veterans needed the bonus now, Congress drew up a new bill to make the pay date earlier.

Sorry, No Bonus!

To show support for the proposed bill, about twenty thousand veterans, who came to be called the Bonus Army, traveled to Washington, D.C., where they set up a camp near the Anacostia River. But the veterans' hopes were dashed when the Senate defeated the bill. Naturally, the veterans were angry. They decided to stay in Washington to protest.

President Herbert Hoover would not stand for this. The police, who were sent to clear out the veterans, killed two men. Then, to make sure that all the veterans would go, Hoover had General Douglas MacArthur send in the United States Army. The troops destroyed what was left of the veterans' camp. In the process, they accidentally killed an eleven-month-old baby with tear gas. Many Americans were disgusted by the government's betrayal of the veterans and by Hoover's insensitivity.

The Bonus Army (opposite) wanted the bonus veterans were due to receive for their service in World War I to be paid early, to help former military men feed their families through the Great Depression. Their demands were eventually met with violence (above), causing many Americans to doubt the Hoover administration's compassion for those who were suffering. Many thought Hoover had turned a deaf ear to the popular song of the time, "Brother, Can You Spare a Dime?"

35

The Hawley-Smoot Tariff

At first, President Herbert Hoover hoped the economy would eventually fix itself. He considered the Depression a natural cycle in business. When events proved him wrong, Hoover took action. He signed the Hawley-Smoot Tariff Act into law on June 17, 1930, hoping that raising tariffs on imported goods would increase the market share for American products. (A tariff is a fee paid on goods imported or exported, often used to encourage consumers to buy domestic products.) Unfortunately, Hawley-Smoot caused America's trading partners to raise tariffs on American goods as well, causing a falloff in American exports. In turn, production had to decrease and more jobs were lost. Hawley-Smoot was also a final blow to many American farmers who could no longer export their produce. Hoover would try other policies to fix the problems being caused by the Great Depression, but it would take another president to succeed.

A New Deal for America

Americans were tired of Hoover's Republican administration and they voted for change—for the Democratic candidate, Franklin Delano Roosevelt. At his inauguration on March 4, 1933, Roosevelt told the American people, "The only thing we have to fear is fear itself. . . . This nation asks for action, and action now. We must act and act quickly." President Roosevelt made it clear to his Cabinet that they had to experiment with new ideas to solve the problems of the Depression. If one approach did not work, they must try something else.

Roosevelt's actions would forever change the role of American government. Roosevelt's collection of federal government programs, known as the New Deal, was aimed at reviving the economy and putting Americans back to work. In responding to the needs

IT IS EVOLUTION, NOT REVOLUTION, GENTLEMEN!

The Roosevelt administration put so many new agencies, usually called by their initials, into effect that his system of government was sometimes referred to as "alphabet soup." Some critics complained that many of Roosevelt's New Deal agencies did little more than create needless work for people and put the United States on a slippery slope toward socialism, as seen in this cartoon (above).

of the ordinary American, New Deal legislation increased the power and size of the federal government. Ironically, many New Deal programs were modeled on policies Hoover and his so-called "do nothing" administration had tried first. Roosevelt advisor Rexford Tugwell later said, "We didn't admit it at the time [1933], but practically the whole New Deal was extrapolated [taken] from programs that Hoover started."

One of Roosevelt's first acts in office was to declare a nationwide weeklong bank holiday. During this time, withdrawals were banned, the United States Treasury Department examined the banks' books, and Congress passed the Emergency Banking Relief Act. The president now had the power to regulate banking transactions. Nine thousand banks had failed by 1933 and 9 million savings accounts had been wiped out. Customers panicked by rumors of bank problems withdrew all their money, forcing the banks, which lacked the money to pay what they owed to all their customers, to close. To reassure the public and to gain support for his actions, Roosevelt gave a "fireside chat" on the radio. Later in 1933, the government created the Federal Deposit

Although the Supreme Court seemed to despise the NRA, many Americans greatly approved of any effort to put people back to work and to aid the failing economy. Most were eager to show support for the president's policies (right).

Insurance Corporation (FDIC) to insure deposits up to $5,000 in all national and state banks in the Federal Reserve System.

Among the many important New Deal programs was the Civilian Conservation Corps (CCC). It provided jobs for about 2 million young men. The jobs involved the preservation of the environment through such measures as planting trees. The AAA helped farmers. The WPA made construction jobs available, as well as work for artists. The Federal Emergency Relief Administration (FERA) funded state programs. The Tennessee Valley Authority (TVA) was set up to build dams and produce electricity in the impoverished Tennessee Valley.

One of the most controversial programs was the National Industrial Recovery Act (NIRA), administered by the National Recovery Administration (NRA), which had the power to regulate competition and labor practices, set minimum wages, and stabilize prices. Of course, many businesses opposed the NRA. And in 1935, the United States Supreme Court, declaring that the Roosevelt administration and Congress had exceeded their authority, declared the NRA unconstitutional. However, Roosevelt was reelected in 1936, and he managed to reinstate some of the NRA's main ideas in later New Deal laws.

"Which Side Are You On?"

The words of Florence Reece's famous union song "Which Side Are You On?" called upon America's workers to choose sides in the ongoing battle between labor and management. And choose sides they did. In the 1930s, as never before, working people developed a sense of solidarity. There was a shared sense of anger and resentment at the capitalist system that had brought on the Great Depression. Union membership soared as workers sought to protect their jobs and participated in strikes for better working conditions. Others, identifying the wealthy and powerful as their class enemies, were inspired by the social progress and fairer distribution of wealth they believed was occurring in the Communist Soviet Union. Known as progressives, they joined leftist political organizations such as the Communist party or the Socialist party. (Communists believed that the government should own all property, distributing money and other goods to people according to their needs. Socialists were less radical, believing that the government should take steps to regulate the way businesses were run, in order to protect the working people.) It seemed to many that the only way to improve life in America would be to replace the capitalist system with a different one.

President Roosevelt was determined to make the existing capitalist system work to fill the needs of America's workers. He introduced legislation in support of unionization, and in 1935, Congress passed the National Labor Relations Act (NLRA). Now labor was

Although traditional conservative Republicans opposed the New Deal and especially programs such as Social Security (below), accusing the government of interfering with private enterprise and infringing on individual freedom, the programs helped pull the economy out of the most severe slump in its history.

39

STEEL WORKERS
ORGANIZING COMMITTEE
Affiliated with C.I.O.

During the 1930s, as workers were faced with the possibility of sudden unemployment and terrible poverty, it became more important than ever to fight for better working conditions. As a result, union activity became common among all types of workers, such as these steel workers (above) in Pennsylvania.

guaranteed the right to unionize, and companies were forbidden to try to break up unions. The labor movement grew stronger when labor leader John L. Lewis, president of the United Mine Workers of America (UMWA), left the American Federation of Labor (AFL) to form the Congress of Industrial Organizations (CIO) because the AFL would not admit unskilled workers. In 1936 and 1937, the CIO organized a wave of successful sit-down strikes involving about half a million workers in the automobile and steel industries. Folk singers such as Woody Guthrie traveled around the country, singing songs about the unions and the struggles of working people. By the end of the decade, nearly all of America's major industries were unionized.

Last Hired, First Fired

If life during the Great Depression was difficult for many white Americans, it was even worse for African Americans. While discrimination was nothing new to African Americans, job discrimination during the 1930s was especially severe, in the North as well as in the South. When employers needed to reduce the number of their employees, African Americans were usually the first to be fired. And because of racial prejudice, many employers, given the choice, preferred to hire an inexperienced white over an experienced African American whenever they had a position to fill. Other minorities had troubles, too. Some four hundred thousand Mexican Americans, for example, faced deportation to Mexico during the 1930s because of job pressures. Whites, who preferred not to compete with recent immigrants for job openings, simply forced these people to return to their original home.

Unemployed whites took jobs that they would have avoided in the past, considering them too menial, such as garbage collector, street sweeper, or elevator operator. In so doing, they took away the only jobs that many African Americans had ever done. Also, many families could no longer afford to hire servants, which put many African-American women out of work.

In 1932, the unemployment rate for African Americans stood at an average of 48 percent compared with about 25 percent for whites. In some places, the unemployment rate for African Americans was much higher—for example, 70 percent in the city of Pittsburgh, Pennsylvania. By 1932, churches and private charities that had been providing a bare minimum level of relief to African-American families had used up their resources.

Fortunately, the early New Deal programs were able to help African Americans by providing food, shelter, clothing, and jobs. The CCC hired black youths to work in integrated conservation camps. The National Youth Administration (NYA) provided student relief programs that allowed young African-American men and women to stay in school. The WPA's Federal Art Project provided jobs for African-American artists and taught almost a quarter of a million blacks to read and write. And the Public Works Administration (PWA) reserved more than one third of the housing units it built for African Americans.

African Americans, who were generally the first fired and the last hired during times of economic strife, faced especially terrible situations during the Great Depression. Discrimination extended beyond the workplace and into everyday society, where African Americans were still denied their civil rights. Thanks to the efforts of civil rights lawyers such as Thurgood Marshall (below), African Americans later made great strides toward equality.

The Roosevelt administration also acted in other ways to help African Americans. President Roosevelt sought the advice of civil rights activists such as Walter White, the head of the National Association for the Advancement of Colored People (NAACP); union leader A. Philip Randolph; Mary McLeod Bethune; and others. Roosevelt's unofficial "black cabinet" would become the Federal Council on Negro Affairs, headed by Mary Bethune.

First Lady Eleanor Roosevelt gave speeches, made radio broadcasts, and wrote newspaper editorials for the cause of racial equality. She helped secure positions for African Americans in the Roosevelt administration, tripling the number of blacks working for the federal government. And in 1939, she resigned from the Daughters of the American Revolution (DAR) because the organization had refused to allow African-American opera singer Marian Anderson to perform at Washington's Constitution Hall, which was owned by the DAR.

Asa Philip Randolph (above) was a leader in the struggle for civil rights from the 1920s through the 1960s. He was also a leading figure in the labor movement. He founded the Brotherhood of Sleeping Car Porters, which he headed until 1968. In 1957, he would become a vice president of the American Federation of Labor and Congress of Industrial Organizations (AFL-CIO).

Not Our Problem— Isolationism in America

During the 1930s, the world was becoming an increasingly more dangerous place. Fascist dictators were drawing up plans for territorial conquest, and before long, their armies would be on the march. Wars would break out in various places overseas and would eventually threaten to engulf more and more nations. But the majority of Americans during the 1930s, preoccupied with trying to survive the Depression, had no desire to get involved in problems overseas. Isolationist sentiment was so strong in America that the United States had never even become a member of the League of Nations formed after World War I, whose purpose was to keep peace in the world.

Secure in the knowledge that two very wide oceans separated the United States from Europe and Asia, most Americans were isolationists. They wanted to sit back and look the other way as the rest of the world fell apart. This would be impossible, however, because of America's economic interests abroad.

To the west, on the other side of the Pacific Ocean, Japan had invaded and occupied Manchuria in northern China in 1931, setting up a puppet government. The Japanese military had taken control of Japan's civilian government, blaming it for the Depression that was affecting not only the United States but the entire world. The military kept Emperor Hirohito as head of state, thus winning popular support for its actions. The League of Nations condemned Japan's aggression but was powerless to stop it, and in 1933, Japan withdrew from the league. The Japanese planned to conquer the rest of China, and in 1937, they embarked on an all-out war of aggression against China. Japan intended to establish a Pacific empire.

To the east, across the Atlantic Ocean, brutal Fascist dictators were in control of Italy and Germany, and anyone paying attention to developments there would have had good reason to fear the worst. Italy's Benito Mussolini, who had come to power in 1922, was envious of the British

Emperor Hirohito (below) remained silent during Japan's military aggression in the 1930s. In so doing, he approved many of the decisions that ultimately led to World War II.

43

Mussolini (above) hoped to make Italy a great power with a vast colonial empire. He invaded and conquered Ethiopia, Africa, during 1935 and 1936. When this invasion was condemned by Great Britain, France, and other European countries, Mussolini entered an alliance with German dictator Adolf Hitler. Mussolini would join Hitler in sending armies to fight in the Spanish Civil War in support of General Francisco Franco in 1936.

and French colonial empires in Africa. Hoping to carve out an Italian empire in Africa, in 1935 Mussolini ordered an invasion of Ethiopia. In 1936, Ethiopia's exiled emperor Haile Selassie appealed to the League of Nations for help, warning, "It is us today. It will be you tomorrow." But the league did nothing.

Meanwhile, in Germany, Adolf Hitler and his National Socialist German Workers' (Nazi) party were in power. Hitler, who had been named chancellor (chief executive officer) of Germany in 1933, assumed total power in 1934 when President Paul Ludwig von Hindenburg died. Hitler, who believed minorities, especially Jews, were inferior to Germans, or Aryans, took control of every aspect of German life. He began to pass laws that deprived German Jews of most of their rights. Hitler's Gestapo murdered hundreds of the Nazis' political opponents. But most Germans, impressed with Hitler's success in putting Germans back to work and rebuilding Germany's devastated economy, gave him their support. Indeed, they were delighted with their new highways and the rebuilding of Germany's armed forces. And they were especially thrilled by their *führer*'s (leader's) strong speeches at mass rallies and on the radio. They listened spellbound as Hitler proclaimed the birth of Germany's Third Reich (empire), which he said would last for at least a thousand years.

Soon Hitler was ready to test the resolve of the other major European powers—France and Great Britain. And unfortunately, the desire of those two nations to keep the peace in Europe would lead them to adopt a policy of

appeasement (giving in) toward Hitler that would ultimately lead to a world war. Hitler was determined to defy the Treaty of Versailles, which Germany and the Allies had signed in 1919, ending World War I. The treaty had required Germany to accept full responsibility for the war and to pay huge war reparations (debts paid as punishment) to the victors. These payments had wrecked the German economy in the 1920s. Hitler ignored the treaty's prohibition against rebuilding Germany's armed forces. And in March 1936, Hitler sent his troops to occupy the Rhineland, a thirty-mile-wide area of Germany bordering France, which, according to the treaty, was to remain free from military use. France and Great Britain did nothing about it. Hitler was encouraged by this. By October 1936, Germany, Italy, and Japan had become allies known as the Axis Powers.

From 1933 on, Hitler (above) busily got Germany ready for war. At first, he worked secretly to rearm the nation. Then, as he saw that no other nations were opposing him, he began to arm Germany in clear violation of the Treaty of Versailles. Still, no other nation tried to stop him. Hitler then laid plans to make Germany the world's greatest power—and to exterminate the Jewish people.

Dictatorship in the Soviet Union

In the Soviet Union, Communist dictator Joseph Stalin strengthened his iron-fisted rule by executing many high-ranking military officers and Communist party officials during a five-year-long purge of those Stalin considered enemies of the state. He also sent as many as 10 million Soviet citizens to labor camps in Siberia, where many died. Also during the 1930s, Stalin forced Soviet

farms to collectivize, or join together under the common ownership of the government. This change in traditional farming caused widespread famine when the central government's agricultural plans failed.

On December 21, 1879, the future dictator Joseph Stalin (above) was born as Iosif Vissarionovich Djugashvili. In 1913, he adopted the name "Stalin" from a Russian word that means man of steel. When the first leader of the Soviet Union, Vladimir Lenin, died in 1924, Stalin worked to build his own power and to destroy his enemies. By December 1929, Stalin had become a dictator.

Dress Rehearsal for War

In July 1936 in Spain, General Francisco Franco, who had won the support of Spanish military leaders, set out to overthrow the country's democratically elected government. His goal was to do away with the republic and establish a Fascist dictatorship with himself in charge. Franco's revolt would result in three years of civil war.

In January 1937, the war was a stalemate. Neither the Loyalists, who supported the democratic government, nor Franco's Nationalist Fascists could gain the upper hand. The United States Congress had passed a Neutrality Act forbidding the sale of arms to either side. Hitler and Mussolini, however, had no such laws restraining them. By April 1937, one hundred thousand Italian soldiers were fighting in Spain for the Nationalists. And Hitler sent his Condor Legion, a unit of warplanes, to help defeat the Loyalists. On April 27, the Condor Legion bombed the city of Guernica, Spain, destroying the town and killing sixteen hundred of its citizens. Spanish painter Pablo Picasso created a huge painting called *Guernica* in response to this outrageous act.

Not all Americans were isolationists. At least three thousand idealistic young American men believed the time had come to stand up to the Fascists. They went to Spain, where they fought for the Loyalist cause as

members of the Abraham Lincoln Brigade. Also in Spain, to report on the war, were the American writers Ernest Hemingway and John Dos Passos. Both were Loyalist supporters. Unfortunately, the Loyalists were greatly outnumbered and outgunned, and in 1939, Franco became the dictator of Spain. In 1940, Hemingway published his novel *For Whom the Bell Tolls*, about the Spanish Civil War.

Hitler's War Against the Jews

Hitler blamed the Jews for all of Germany's problems. Because he was such an effective speaker, he convinced millions of Germans that he was right—that the Jews did not even deserve to be treated as human beings. Hitler's Nuremberg Laws of 1935 deprived German Jews of their citizenship. Jewish books were burned.

Born Francisco Franco Bahamonde in the province of La Coruna, Franco (above, at lower right) was dictator of Spain from 1939 until his death in 1975. During the Spanish Civil War (above), Franco led the rebel Nationalist Army, aided by Italian troops and German warplanes, to victory over the Loyalist (Republican) forces, who were aided by many foreign soldiers, including some Americans. After his victory, Franco took control of Spain as a dictator, calling himself El Caudillo (the leader).

The excuse used by the Nazis for justifying the start of the campaign of terror known as Kristallnacht (above) was the murder of Ernst Von Rath. Von Rath was a high-ranking official in the German Embassy in Paris, France. He had been killed by a teenage German Jewish refugee.

Jewish Germans could no longer marry or do business with non-Jewish Germans. Jewish professionals were fired from their jobs. Life for German Jews steadily grew worse. Those who could, made plans to leave Germany.

On the night of November 9, 1938, mobs of Germans, organized by the Nazis, attacked Jews throughout Germany and Austria. Thousands of Jewish synagogues, homes, and businesses were burned. Hundreds of Jews were beaten and dozens were killed. More than thirty thousand Jews were arrested. Because of the shattered windows in Jewish buildings and the shards of glass littering the streets, the night came to be known as *Kristallnacht* (Night of Broken Glass).

Before long, the Nazis began rounding up Jews in Germany, Austria, and other Nazi-occupied countries, and sending them to concentration camps where they were held as prisoners and forced to do grueling labor. Hitler eventually announced his "Final Solution" to the so-called Jewish problem—all Jews were to be killed. The concentration camps became death camps. In the early 1940s, about 6 million Jews would be systematically murdered in the concentration camps. The worst genocidal episode in history, this would come to be called the Holocaust.

Throughout the 1930s, Hitler's persecution of the Jews was reported in the news in America and elsewhere. Most Americans were appalled—but not all. Unfortunately, anti-Semitism (anti-Jewish sentiment) did not exist in Germany alone. In America, there were many who supported Hitler's actions. By 1939, there were more than eight hundred Fascist and anti-Semitic organizations in the United States, among them the German-American Bund and "radio priest" Father Charles Coughlin's National Union for Social Justice.

The Trouble With Appeasement

The French wanted peace. The English wanted peace. The horrors of World War I were still fresh in many minds. So when Hitler made a demand, the British and French gave in, hoping to preserve peace. That is why Great Britain and France accepted Hitler's *Anschluss* (annexation) of Austria on March 12, 1938. It is also why British Prime Minister Neville Chamberlain, on September 29 and 30 in Munich, agreed to Hitler's occupation of the Sudetenland, a Czech province inhabited mostly by Germans. With each of his demands, Hitler gave the impression that he would be satisfied and would make no further demands. But each time Hitler got what he wanted, his appetite for more territory grew stronger. In fact, he ignored the promises he made in the Munich Agreement to limit his territorial seizures. Hitler had made his desire for *lebensraum* (living space) perfectly clear, so his attempt to win more territory was not too surprising.

When Chamberlain returned to England from Munich, he told the cheering crowds that were on hand to greet him, "I believe it is peace in our time." But Winston Churchill, who would lead Great Britain during the war to come, said Munich

represented "a total and unmitigated defeat." It was only the beginning—Hitler would soon want more.

Within six months, Hitler's troops took over all of Czechoslovakia. Mussolini, inspired by Hitler's success, invaded and occupied Albania. Next on Hitler's list was Poland. Although England and France had said they would guarantee Poland's independence, by this time Hitler had nothing but contempt for the British and French. He assumed they would not act. This time, however, he was wrong.

On August 23, 1939, Hitler and Soviet dictator Joseph Stalin signed a nonaggression pact. Hitler and Stalin secretly agreed to divide Poland between them. The world was shocked by this

World War II began when invading German troops marched through Poland in September 1939 (opposite). The war would last until the mid-1940s and would eventually include a huge number of the world's nations.

In 1939, Soviet leader Joseph Stalin signed a nonaggression pact with Adolf Hitler, each promising not to attack the other. Above, Soviet Foreign Commissar Vyacheslav Molotov signs the agreement as Stalin and Joachim von Ribbentrop, Hitler's top diplomatic officer, look on.

sudden turn of events. At the time, Stalin had been negotiating with Great Britain and France in the hopes of stopping Hitler's aggression. Stalin's action was especially shocking to those progressive idealists in America who had great respect for the Soviet Union's Communist system.

On September 1, 1939, Hitler's troops invaded Poland in a massive surprise attack. Two days later, Great Britain and France declared war on Germany. World War II, which would change the decade to come—and the world—forever, had begun.

The Discovery of Planet X

Astronomers had long suspected that the solar system contained another planet beyond the eight known planets—Mercury, Venus, Earth, Mars, Jupiter, Saturn, Uranus, and Neptune. Careful mathematical calculations of the orbit of the planet Neptune led astronomers to believe that Neptune was being influenced by the gravitational pull of another planet even farther away from the sun. Among those predicting the existence of "Planet X" was astronomer Percival Lowell. After Lowell's death, young astronomer Clyde W. Tombaugh took up the search. Working at Lowell Observatory in Flagstaff, Arizona, Tombaugh, on February 18, 1930, photographed the tiny mysterious planet close to its predicted location. "Planet X" was given a name from mythology—Pluto, the Greek god of the underworld.

Pluto (above) is one of the coldest places in our solar system. It travels around the sun in an oval-shaped orbit. As it orbits the sun, Pluto spins on its axis, spinning around once in about six Earth days. Pluto's estimated diameter is about 1,430 miles, less than a fifth the size of Earth.

Buildings, Bridges, and Dams

Throughout the Depression years, a succession of mighty structures was completed all around America. These feats of engineering, making use of the latest building technologies, were symbols of progress that cheered Americans, at least for a while. In New York City, the world's tallest skyscraper—the 102-story, 1,250-foot-high Empire State Building—opened on May 1, 1931, having been built in less than two years. The building's architect, R. H. Shreve, claimed that, although the building weighed 600 million pounds, because of its placement on 220 columns, its impact on the earth beneath it was equal to that of a 45-foot-high

The Empire State Building (opposite), designed by the architectural firm of Shreve, Lamb & Harmon, was the world's tallest building until the 1970s. Today, only the Sears Tower in Chicago and the World Trade Center in New York are taller. The building is a fine example of art deco, a style that was very popular during the 1920s and 1930s.

53

Designed by Joseph B. Strauss and built for a cost of about $35.5 million, the Golden Gate Bridge (opposite) is an 8,981-foot-long suspension bridge. Its towers, measuring about 1,120 feet, are some of the first structures that can be seen by ships as they approach the city of San Francisco.

pile of rock. The building contained 10 million bricks, 2.5 million feet of electric wire, 50 miles of radiator pipe, 3,500 miles of telephone and telegraph cable, and 67 elevators placed within 7 miles of elevator shaft. The Empire State Building attracted the attention of movie-goers in 1933 when the film *King Kong* showed the giant ape climbing up the outside of the building. Millions of visitors during the 1930s had an uplifting experience riding the Empire State Building's elevators into the sky above Manhattan. But unfortunately, although 2 million square feet of office space was available, the Empire State Building remained mostly vacant for many years because most businesses during the Great Depression could not afford the rent.

Magnificent new bridges were also completed during the 1930s. In New York, the George Washington Bridge (1931) spanned the Hudson River from Manhattan to Fort Lee, New Jersey. It was suspended from great towers of steel and swayed with the wind. The Triborough Bridge system (1936) linked the boroughs of Manhattan, Queens, and the Bronx. On the other side of the country, the eight-mile-long San Francisco–Oakland Bay Bridge (1936) connected San Francisco and Oakland, California, and the Golden Gate Bridge (1937) joined San Francisco and the Marin Headlands. More than a quarter of a million people walked across the Golden Gate Bridge on October 1, 1937, the day it opened.

In the Southwest, a huge dam was built on the Colorado River to provide electricity to places such as Los Angeles and to control flooding. The construction of Boulder Dam began in September 1930. The project, finished in 1936, created hundreds of jobs. Unfortunately, many workers died of heat exhaustion under the broiling

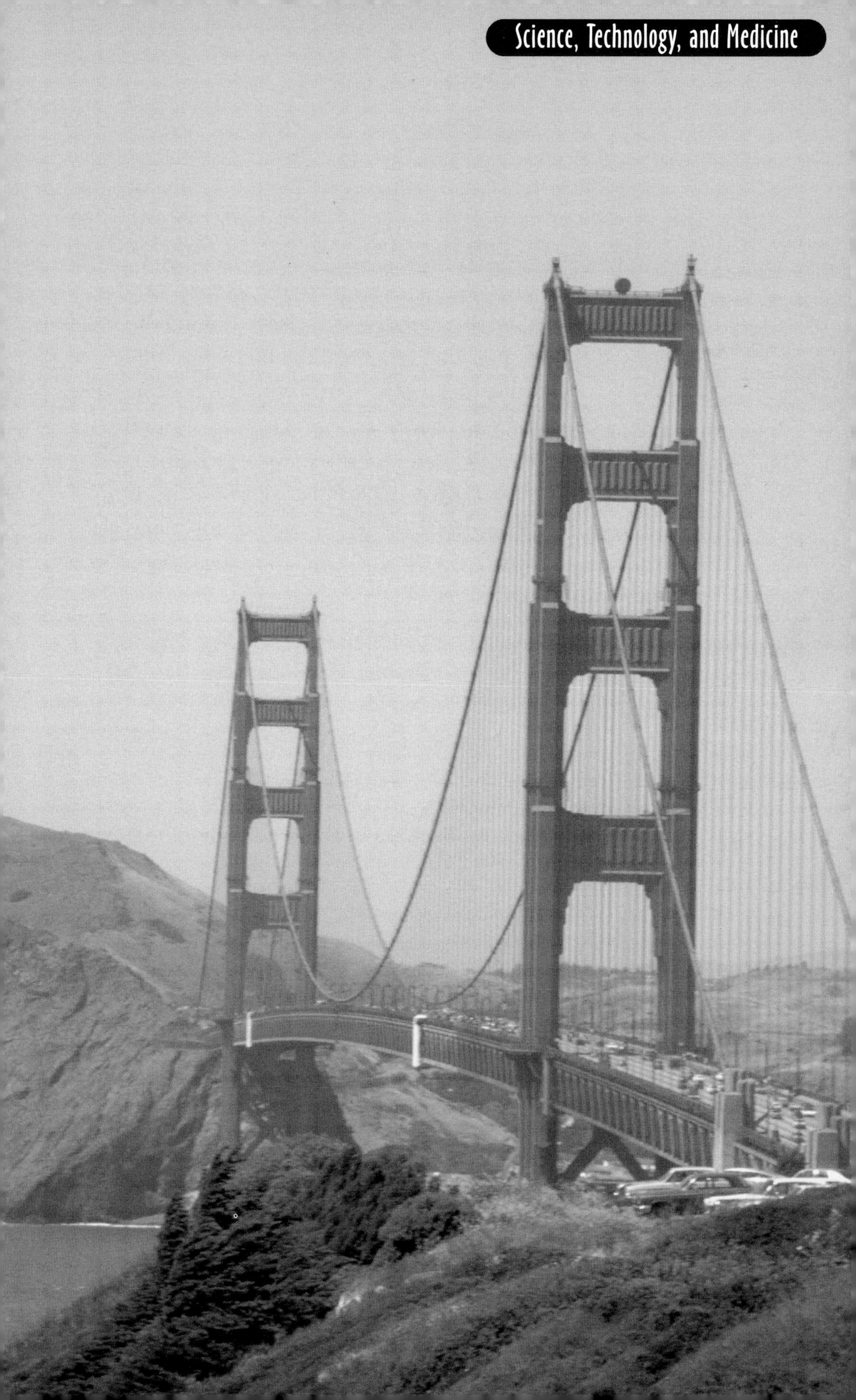

desert sun. The 725-foot-high Boulder Dam, one of the tallest dams in the world, created 115-mile-long Lake Mead. Because Herbert Hoover, as secretary of commerce, played a big role in planning and funding the project, the dam was later officially renamed Hoover Dam.

Passenger Airships

For a brief period in the 1930s, it seemed that a new type of passenger transportation had arrived—the rigid airship known as the dirigible or zeppelin, named after Count Ferdinand von Zeppelin, the German engineer who developed it. In 1936, the 804-foot-long, hydrogen-filled German airship *Hindenburg* began making flights across the Atlantic Ocean. It could carry as many as fifty passengers and a crew of about fifty in comfort. As the giant airship floated silently across the sky, high above the ocean waves, passengers enjoyed an experience comparable to being on a luxury ocean liner. The trip from Germany to New Jersey usually took fifty to sixty hours and cost $400 one way, $720 round trip. By May 1937, the *Hindenburg* had made thirty-six trips across the ocean. Plans were being made to build more airships and to begin regular transatlantic flights. But on May 6, 1937, disaster struck. As the *Hindenburg* prepared

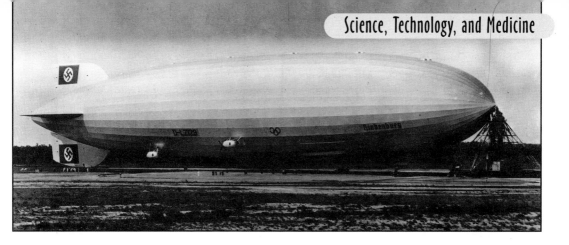

to land at Lakehurst, New Jersey, the hydrogen inside exploded and the zeppelin burst into flames. Thirty-six people were killed. Sadly, the age of the passenger airship came to a sudden close.

Wonder Drugs

"Wonder drugs!" That's what people called the new sulfa drugs. Sulfa drugs, or sulfonamides, were the first drugs to fight bacterial infections such as scarlet fever and meningitis successfully. In 1932, German biochemist Gerhard Domagk noticed that a red dye known as Prontosil cured certain infections in laboratory mice. Researchers in Paris investigated Prontosil and found that its active ingredient was sulfonamide. American researchers at Johns Hopkins Hospital did clinical research and found that Prontosil was effective against bacterial organisms such as streptococcus, meningococcus, and gonococcus. Sulfonamides would later be used as the first antibiotics, fighting illnesses that had long plagued people all over the world and saving countless lives.

One of the biggest aircrafts ever built, the Hindenburg (above) had a volume of 7 million cubic feet and flew at 78 miles an hour. On the day it exploded, it carried ninety-seven people, thirty-five of whom were killed, along with a member of the ground crew. After the disaster, rigid airships were no longer being developed.

An Amazing Decade

The decade of the 1930s was, for many Americans, the most difficult time of their lives. For many people facing the scary prospect of no longer having a job, it was a question of survival. How would they eat? Where would they sleep? Many wondered whether the shattered economy would ever revive. Some people began to think that perhaps the capitalist system itself was in need of replacement.

The Roosevelt administration and its New Deal programs helped bring the country through the Great Depression, with the many new agencies designed to help ordinary people and to provide jobs for those who were out of work. But ultimately, it would take World War II in the 1940s, fought to combat fascism in Europe and Asia, to restore the American economy.

The Great Depression touched the lives of Americans from all classes of society. Suffering was great among the poor and the unemployed, and especially among farmers and migrant workers (opposite and below), who faced not only a sinking economy, but the ravages of the Dust Bowl. At first, some politicians, such as Republican Dwight Morrow, thought the downswing was good. In October 1930, Morrow remarked, "There is something about too much prosperity that ruins the fiber of the people." By the time President Franklin Roosevelt came to the presidency, however, times had become even worse. People were grateful for the assistance his New Deal programs offered. The New Deal established a precedent of government activism on behalf of all the people, including the most disadvantaged.

1929—Stock market crashes; Great Depression begins.

1930—On February 18, Clyde Tombaugh photographs the planet that will become known as Pluto; President Hoover (left) promises on March 7 that the Depression will be over in sixty days; On June 17, Hoover signs Hawley-Smoot Tariff into law; In September, construction begins on Boulder (later Hoover) Dam; In the fall, Hoover creates the President's Emergency Committee for Employment (PECE); *Little Caesar* opens in theaters.

1931—In May, Hoover says allowing the government to provide Depression relief will hurt the character of the American people; *The Public Enemy* premieres in theaters; *Dracula* (left) and *Frankenstein* premiere; Scottsboro boys are arrested on rape charges; Japan occupies Manchuria; On May 1, the Empire State Building opens in New York City; The George Washington Bridge, linking New York City and New Jersey, opens.

1932—On March 1, the Lindbergh baby is kidnapped; Babe Didrikson wins two gold medals and sets hurdle records in the Olympics; Bonus Army marches on Washington, D.C., and is met with violence from government forces; German biochemist Gerhard Domagk finds that Prontosil cures infections in laboratory mice; In November, Franklin D. Roosevelt is elected president.

1933—President Franklin Roosevelt is inaugurated on March 4; Roosevelt sets up the Agricultural Adjustment Administration (AAA); Prohibition is repealed; The Chicago World's Fair begins; *King Kong*, *42nd Street*, *Flying Down to Rio*, and *Duck Soup* premiere in theaters; Roosevelt administration creates the Federal Deposit Insurance Corporation (FDIC); Japan withdraws from the League of Nations; Adolf Hitler (left) becomes chancellor of Germany.

1934—Shirley Temple (below left) has her first starring role in *Stand Up and Cheer*; *The Thin Man* premieres; President von Hindenburg dies and Adolf Hitler assumes complete control over the German government.

1935—Amelia Earhart makes the first flight from Hawaii to California; Soil Conservation Service (SCS) is established; Bingo is introduced; Monopoly is introduced; First chain letters appear in the mail; *Mutiny on the Bounty* premieres; The United States Supreme Court declares the National

Recovery Administration unconstitutional; Mussolini orders an Italian invasion of Ethiopia; Nuremberg Laws deprive German Jews of many rights.

1936—Bruno Richard Hauptmann (top right) is executed for the murder of the Lindbergh baby; Jesse Owens and other African-American athletes win eight gold, three silver, and two bronze medals at the Olympic Games in Munich; In July, General Francisco Franco (right) begins the Spanish Civil War when he attempts to overthrow the government; The Triborough Bridge, linking Manhattan, Queens, and the Bronx, opens; In November, Franklin Roosevelt is reelected president; CIO begins a wave of labor strikes; Ethiopian emperor Haile Selassie appeals to the League of Nations to help remove Italian forces from Ethiopia; Hitler's forces occupy the Rhineland; Germany, Italy, and Japan form the Axis Powers.

1937—Amelia Earhart disappears while on a flight around the world; Japan begins war with China; During the fighting in the Spanish Civil War, Hitler's Condor Legion bombs the city of Guernica; The Golden Gate Bridge (below right) opens, linking San Francisco and Marin County, California; On May 6, the *Hindenburg* explodes over New Jersey.

1938—On March 12, Hitler annexes Austria; Walt Disney releases *Snow White and the Seven Dwarfs*; In September, British Prime Minister Neville Chamberlain and Hitler sign the Munich Agreement; On October 30, Orson Welles's (bottom right) radio broadcast of *The War of the Worlds* leads people to believe Martians have invaded Earth; On November 9, the *Kristallnacht* attack on Jews takes place in Germany and Austria; Hitler takes over Czechoslovakia; Mussolini invades Albania.

1939—*The Grapes of Wrath* is published; The New York World's Fair begins, at which the television is introduced; *My Little Chickadee*, *Stagecoach*, *The Wizard of Oz*, and *Gone With the Wind* open in theaters; Billie Holiday records "Strange Fruit"; Francisco Franco becomes dictator of Spain; On August 23, Hitler and Stalin sign a nonaggression pact; On September 1, Hitler's troops invade Poland, starting World War II.

Further Reading

Evans, Harold. *The American Century*. New York: Alfred A. Knopf, 1998.

Fremon, David K. *The Great Depression in American History*. Springfield, N.J.: Enslow Publishers, Inc., 1996.

Gerdes, Louise I. *The 1930s*. San Diego, Calif.: Greenhaven Press, 2000.

Jennings, Peter, and Todd Brewster. *The Century*. New York: Doubleday, 1998.

Junior Chronicle of the 20th Century. New York: DK Publishing, 1997.

Spies, Karen Bornemann. *Franklin D. Roosevelt*. Springfield, N.J.: Enslow Publishers, Inc., 1999.

Stewart, Gail B. *1930s*. Parsippany, N.J.: Silver Burdett Press, 1989.

Internet Addresses

American Studies @ UVA. *1930s Project*. n.d. <http://xroads.virginia.edu/~1930s/home_1.html> (September 15, 2000).

Haven, Janet. *The Hoover Dam: Lonely Lands Made Fruitful*. n.d. <http://xroads.virginia.edu/~MA98/haven/hoover/front2.html> (September 15, 2000).

Hunterdon Online. *The Lindbergh Case*. 1999. <http://www.lindberghtrial.com/html/front.shtml> (September 15, 2000).

Library of Congress. "America from the Great Depression to World War II." *American Memory*. December 15, 1998. <http://memory.loc.gov/ammem/fsowhome.html> (September 15, 2000).

PBS Online. "Riding the Rails." *The American Experience*. 1999. <http://www.pbs.org/wgbh/amex/rails/> (September 15, 2000).

White House Historical Association. "Franklin D. Roosevelt." *The Presidents*. n.d. <http://www.whitehouse.gov/history/presidents/fr32.html> (September 15, 2000).